be the difference

Compiled by Dan Zadra
Designed by Steve Potter and Jenica Wilkie

COMPENDIUM™
INCORPORATED

live inspired.

ACKNOWLEDGEMENTS

These quotations were gathered lovingly but unscientifically over several years and/or were contributed by many friends or acquaintances. Some arrived—and survived in our files—on scraps of paper and may therefore be imperfectly worded or attributed. To the authors, contributors and original sources, our thanks, and where appropriate, our apologies. –The Editors

WITH SPECIAL THANKS TO THE ENTIRE COMPENDIUM FAMILY.

CREDITS
Compiled by: Dan Zadra
Designed by: Steve Potter & Jenica Wilkie

There's always one moment in life when the door opens and lets the future in.

—GRAHAM GREENE

bethe**difference**

**When we do the best we can,
we never know what miracle is wrought
in our life, or in the life of another.**

—HELEN KELLER

We all know the names of the tyrants who terrorize their countries, or the greedy executives who bring down their companies. We know their names because, in a world of 7 billion you's and me's, they are the exceptions—and the exceptions make the news.

But where are the names and the stories of the people you live and work with every day? We have people in our midst who make a positive difference for all of us—and we often can't see them, don't notice them, don't honor them.

While the worst of the world dominates our attention, the best of the world escapes our gaze.

Not too long ago NASA sent a one-ton payload hurtling across a 7-month, 310-million mile trajectory to a Martian landing site the equivalent size of a postage stamp. Scientists worldwide celebrated the mission as an "amazing feat of galactic engineering that will benefit all mankind." And yet very few people on earth will ever know the names of the 2,000 men and women who accomplished this mission on our behalf.

These are the kinds of "anonymous" people who work behind the scenes in every company and community, yours and mine, to do a lot of little things very, very well. Don't ever think that, just because your name doesn't show up in the headlines, that you don't make a difference. You do.

Dan Zadra

BELIEVEINY

OURDREAMS

*If one is lucky,
a solitary fantasy
can totally transform
one million realities.*
—*Maya Angelou*

The story's about you.
—HORACE

In the heart of each of us,
there is a voice of knowing—a song
or a story that can remind us of what
we most value and long for, what we
have known since we were a child.
—JACK KORNFIELD

If a story is in you,
it has got to come out.
—WILLIAM FAULKNER

bethedifference

To each of us, at certain points of our lives, there come opportunities to rearrange our formulas and assumptions— revisit our dreams.

—LEO BUSCAGLIA

You have to leave the city of your comfort and go into the wilderness of your intuition. What you'll discover will be wonderful. What you'll discover is yourself.

—ALAN ALDA

bethedifference

Listen to your dreams—those are
the sounds no one else can hear.
—KOBI YAMADA

Some people say that
dreaming gets you nowhere in life.
But I say you can't get anywhere
in life without dreaming.
—ROSE ZADRA

I've dreamt in my life
dreams that have...gone through me,
like wine through water, and altered
the color of my mind.
—EMILY BRONTË

bethe**difference**

Your past is not your potential.
In any hour you can choose to
liberate the future.
—MARILYN FERGUSON

Though no one can go back
and make a brand new start,
anyone can start from now and
make a brand new ending.
—CARL BARD

No one else can tell
you what your life's work is,
but it's important that you find it.
There is a part of you that
already knows; affirm that part.
—WILLIS W. HARMAN

bethedifference

**Put your future in
good hands—your own.**
—MARK VICTOR HANSEN

**The best day of your life is
the one on which you decide
your life is your own. No apologies
or excuses. No one to lean on,
rely on, or blame. The gift of life
is yours; it is an amazing journey;
and you alone are responsible
for the quality of it.**
—DAN ZADRA

bethedifference

Believe in something big.
Your life is worth a noble motive.
—WALTER ANDERSON

We all need something to believe
in, something that elicits whole-
hearted enthusiasm.
—HANNAH SENESH

There is, then, a simple answer
to the question, "What is the
purpose of our individual lives?"
They have whatever purpose we
succeed in putting into them.
—A.J. AYER

bethedifference

> Desire is possibility
> seeking expression.
> —RALPH WALDO EMERSON

> Every heart has a
> hidden treasure—a secret wish,
> a silent dream—a special
> goal to hope and long for.
> —JILL WOLF

> I now see my life, not as a slow
> shaping of achievement to fit my
> preconceived purposes, but as the
> gradual discovery of a purpose
> which I did not know.
> —JOANNA FIELD

bethedifference

Don't pray for tasks
equal to your powers; pray for
powers equal to your tasks.
—PHILLIPS BROOKS

You are not called to be a
canary in a cage. You are called
to be an eagle and to fly sun
to sun, over continents.
—HENRY WARD BEECHER

Throw your dreams into space
like a kite, and you do not know
what it will bring back, a new life,
a new friend, a new love,
a new country.
—ANAÏS NIN

bethedifference

There are people who put
their dreams in a little box and say,
"Yes, of course, I've got dreams."
Then they put the box away and bring
it out once in awhile to look in it, and
yep, they're still in there. It takes an
uncommon amount of guts to put your
dreams on the line, to hold them up
and say, "How good or how bad am I?"

—ERMA BOMBECK

For of all sad words of tongue
or pen, The saddest are these:
"It might have been."

—JOHN GREENLEAF WHITTIER

16

bethedifference

**Never have regrets,
follow your heart.**
—HILLARY RICHARDS

**Far away there in the
sunshine are my highest
aspirations. I may not reach them,
but I can look up and see their
beauty, believe in them, and try
to follow where they lead.**
—LOUISA MAY ALCOTT

**You are unique, and if that is
not fulfilled, then something
wonderful has been lost.**
—MARTHA GRAHAM

bethedifference

BELIEVE IN

Think of the world you carry within you.
—Rainer Maria Rilke

We all have gifts that we've
never opened. It's time to open some
of yours. Find your wings!
—DAN ZADRA

For awhile I looked outside
to see what I could make the world
give me, instead of looking inside
to see what was there.
—BELL LIVINGSTONE

There is something in
every one of you that waits
and listens for the sound
of the genuine in yourself.
—HOWARD THURMAN

bethedifference

All the wonders you seek
are within yourself.
—SIR THOMAS BROWN

Always believe that you are a
wonderful, unique person, that
you are a once-in-all-history event.
That it's more than your right,
it's your duty to be who you are.
—MICHAEL NOLAN

The greatest gift you will ever
receive is the gift of loving and
believing in yourself. Guard this
gift with your life. It is the only
thing that will ever truly be yours.
—TIFFANY LOREN ROWE

bethedifference

Be faithful to that which
exists nowhere but in yourself.
—ANDRÉ GIDE

We are all born
originals—why is it so
many of us die copies?
—EDWARD YOUNG

The most enlightened prayer
isn't, "Dear God, send me
someone wonderful," but,
"Dear God, help me realize that
I am someone wonderful."
—MARIANNE WILLIAMSON

bethedifference

Insist on being yourself.
No one can do that better
than you, and no one can ever
tell you you're doing it wrong.

—JAMES COLLIER

Our deepest fear is not that we
are inadequate. Our deepest fear
is that we are powerful beyond
measure. It is our light, not our
darkness that most frightens us.
We ask ourselves, Who am I to be
brilliant, talented, fabulous?
Actually who are you *not* to be?

—MARIANNE WILLIAMSON

bethedifference

Trust yourself. You know more than you think you do.
—DR. BENJAMIN SPOCK

You can explore the universe looking for somebody who is more deserving of your love and affection than you are yourself, and you will not find that person anywhere.
—BUDDHIST SAYING

Follow your bliss, and doors will open for you where you didn't know they were going to be.
—JOSEPH CAMPBELL

bethedifference

Don't wait to be discovered.
—GIL ATKINSON

I've gone through life believing in the strength and competence of others; never in my own. Now, dazzled, I discover that my capacities are real. It's like finding a fortune in the lining of an old coat.
—JOAN MILLS

If I am not for myself, who will be? If I am only for myself, what am I? And if not now, when?
—RABBI HILLEL

bethedifference

Everyone has a unique purpose, do you think you are here by mistake?

—ELI SINGER

People often say that this or that person has not yet found himself. But the self is not something one finds, it is something one creates.

—THOMAS SZASZ

Find your true path. It's so easy to become someone we don't want to be, without even realizing it's happening. We are created by the choices we make every day.

—BERNIE SIEGEL, M.D.

bethedifference

I want you to start a crusade in your life—to dare to be your best.
—WILLIAM DANFORTH

You have to finish yourself—no one but you can make you the complete person you were meant to be. Make the best of this simple, fundamental truth. It has unlimited possibilities.
—STUART LEVINE

How many cares one loses when one decides not to be something, but to be someone.
—COCO CHANEL

bethedifference

We think caged birds sing,
when indeed they cry.
—JOHN WEBSTER

You are the one and
only you that ever was or ever
will be. No one really knows
to what heights you might soar.
Even you will not know until
you spread your wings and fly.
—DAN ZADRA

You are the one who can
stretch your own horizon.
—EDGAR F. MAGNIN

bethedifference

Hell would be if God
were to show me things
I could have accomplished if
only I had believed in myself.

—UNKNOWN

If you hear a voice within
you say, "You cannot paint,"
then by all means paint, and
that voice will be silenced.

—VINCENT VAN GOGH

Do the thing and
you shall have the power.

—RALPH WALDO EMERSON

bethedifference

BELIEVEIN

YOURTEAM

**People are saying,
"I want a company and
a job that values me as
much as I value it. I want
something in my life not
just to invest my time in,
but to believe in."**
—*Anita Roddick*

Part of true success is understanding that there's something bigger and more important than ourselves.
—MARCIA ANN GILLESPIE

Organizations exist only for one purpose: to help people reach greater ends together than they could achieve individually.
—ROBERT H. WATERMAN

bethedifference

> Each of us wants to be treated as a unique and valuable individual, but we each have a simultaneous need to belong to something greater than ourselves.
>
> —"BUILDING COMMUNITY"

33

> We must remember that one determined person can make a significant difference, but a small group of determined people can change the course of history.
>
> —SONIA JOHNSON

bethedifference

One person may supply the idea for a company, community or nation, but what gives the idea its force is a community of dreams.

—ANDRÉ MALRAUX

We can do more than belong, we can participate.

—MAYA ANGELOU

Everyone should believe that he or she has something to give to the organization which cannot otherwise be given.

—MICHAEL NOLAN

bethedifference

You can employ men and
women or hired hands to
work for you, but you will have
to win their hearts to have
them work with you.
—WILLIAM J.H. BOETCKER

Everyone has a unique role.
Everyone, including and perhaps
especially you, is indispensable.
—JEAN RENOIR

bethedifference

Who are the most important
people in the company? Everyone.
—PETE SELLECK

What if we could learn to tap the
wonderful, rich differences among
people? Wouldn't a corporation
that could treasure the uniqueness
of each of its 1,000 employees be
phenomenally powerful?
—TOM PETERS

I note the obvious differences
between each sort and type,
but we are more alike, my friends,
than we are unalike.
—MAYA ANGELOU

bethedifference

Accepting diversity enables us
to see that each of us is needed.
It also enables us to abandon
ourselves to the strengths of others,
acknowledging that we cannot know
or do everything on our own.

—MAX DEPREE

When different talents and ideas
rub up against each other, there is
friction, yes. But also sparks, fire,
light and—eventually—brilliance.

—NANCIE O'NEILL

bethedifference

**Surround yourself with
people who believe you can.**
—DAN ZADRA

**Those you followed passionately,
gladly and zealously have made
you feel like somebody. It wasn't
merely the job title or power—
they somehow made you feel
terrific to be around them.**
—IRWIN FEDERMAN

**Good leaders inspire people
to have confidence in them.
Great leaders inspire people to
have confidence in themselves.**
—SAM EWING

38

bethedifference

People must believe in each other, and feel that it *can* and *must* be done—that way they are enormously strong. We must keep each other's courage up.
—VINCENT VAN GOGH

Loyalty means not that I...believe you are always right. Loyalty means that I share a common ideal with you and that, regardless of minor differences, we fight for it, shoulder to shoulder, confident in one another's good faith, trust, constancy, and affection.
—DR. KARL MENNINGER

bethedifference

The place you are in
needs you today.
—KATHERINE LOGAN

Take your heart to work and ask
the most and best of yourself and
everybody else. Don't let your
special character and spirit—
the true essence of you—don't
let that get beaten down.
—MERYL STREEP

Imagine what will happen if
each of us decides to reach just
a little bit higher, to try just a little
bit harder, to care just a little bit
more. That's the power of one.
—GIL ATKINSON

bethedifference

It takes each of us to make
a difference for all of us.
—JACKIE MUTCHESON

What you do does make a
difference. Every little task in
everyone's morning in-basket
contributes directly to the
achievement of the organization's
greater vision and mission.
—CAROLE JOY

Just as there are no little
people or unimportant lives,
there is no insignificant work.
—ELENA BONNER

bethedifference

The world is before you,
and you need not take it
or leave it as it was
when you came in.
—James Baldwin

BELIEVE**WE**
A**BET**

CANBUILD
TERWORLD

Either we have our dreams
or we live our dreams.
—ZOE KOPLOWITZ

We believe it is a necessity
of our times to translate our
beliefs, our hopes and ideals
into concrete action.
—LENEDRA CAROLL

We must have courage to bet on our
ideas, to take the calculated risk,
and to act. Everyday living requires
courage if life is to be effective
and bring happiness.
—MAXWELL MALTZ

bethedifference

We are called upon to become creators, to make the world new.

—JOHN ELOF BOODIN

We are not passive spectators, but active contestants in the drama of our existence. We need to take responsibility for the kind of life we create for ourselves.

—NATHANIEL BRANDEN, PH.D.

If we were logical, the future might look bleak indeed. But we are more than logical. We are human beings, and we have faith, and we have hope, and we can work.

—JACQUES COUSTEAU

bethedifference

We are not in a position
in which we have nothing to
work with. We already have
capacities, talents, direction,
missions, callings.

—ABRAHAM MASLOW

Only one thing has to
change for us to know happiness
in our lives: where we focus our
attention. The good news is
that we can choose.

—GREG ANDERSON

Truth is all around you.
What matters is where and when
you decide to put your focus.

—ROGER VON OECH

bethedifference

**Just think of something
that would be "wonderful"
if it were only "possible."
Then set out to make it possible.**
—ARMAND HAMMER

**A single idea can transform a life,
a business, a nation, a world.**
—DAN ZADRA

**Imagination is the beginning
of creation. You imagine what
you desire, you will what you
imagine and at last you
create what you will.**
—GEORGE BERNARD SHAW

bethedifference

If you don't like the way
the world is, you change it.
You just do it one step at a time.
—MARIAN WRIGHT EDELMAN

The capacity for hope is the
most significant fact of life.
It provides human beings with
a sense of destination and the
energy to get started.
—NORMAN COUSINS

bethedifference

Determine that the thing
can and shall be done, and
then we shall find the way.
—ABRAHAM LINCOLN

49

This is as true in everyday life
as it is in battle: we are given one
life and the decision is ours whether
to wait for circumstances to make
up our mind, or whether to act
and, in acting, to live.
—GENERAL OMAR BRADLEY

bethedifference

**Commitment is never
an act of moderation.**
—KENNETH G. MILLS

**Progress results only from
the fact that there are some
men and women who refuse to
believe that what they know
to be right cannot be done.**
—RUSSELL DAVENPORT

**We couldn't possibly know
where it would lead, but we
knew it had to be done.**
—BETTY FRIEDAN

bethedifference

Idealists, foolish enough to throw caution to the winds, have advanced mankind and have enriched the world.
—EMMA GOLDMAN

At first people refuse to believe that a strange new thing can be done, then they begin to hope it can be done, then they see it can be done—then it is done and all the world wonders why it was not done centuries ago.
—FRANCES H. BURNETT

bethedifference

You really can change
the world if you care enough.
—MARIAN WRIGHT EDELMAN

Dreams come true;
without that possibility
nature would not incite
us to have them.
—JOHN UPDIKE

The dream is real, my friends.
The failure to make it work
is the unreality.
—TONI CADE BAMBARA

bethedifference

This world is your world.
Take it easy, but take it.
—WOODY GUTHRIE

We need to give ourselves
permission to act out
our dreams and visions—
even if it takes a lifetime.
—VIJALI HAMILTON

Think beyond your lifetime
if you want to accomplish
something truly great.
—WALT DISNEY

bethedifference

There are many wonderful things that will never be done if you do not do them.

—Charles D. Gill

The four great questions:
Why are you here? Where have
you been? Where are you going?
What difference will you make?
—HAL SIMON

We must not, in trying to think
about how we can make a big
difference, ignore the small daily
differences we can make...
—MARIAN WRIGHT EDELMAN

It is exciting to discover the
power that you possess and
have been exercising without
even knowing it.
—MILDRED NEWMAN AND
BERNARD BERKOWITZ

bethedifference

We are all designed
for a specific purpose; we
all have something for which
each of us, and each of us
alone, is responsible.

—NAOMI STEPHAN

There is a vitality, a life-force,
an energy, a quickening that is
translated through you into action.
And because there is only one you in
all time, your expression is unique.
If you block it, it will never exist
through any other medium and
will be lost.

—MARTHA GRAHAM

bethedifference

The purpose of life is to discover your gift. The meaning of life is to give it away.

—DAVID VISCOTT

I believe every person is born with talent. Talent is like electricity. Electricity makes no judgment. You can plug into it and light up a lamp, keep a heart pump going, light a cathedral, or you can electrocute a person with it. It makes no judgment. I think talent is like that.

—MAYA ANGELOU

bethedifference

I seldom think about my limitations, and they never make me sad. Perhaps there is just a touch of yearning at times; but it is vague, like a breeze among flowers.

—HELEN KELLER

Make yourself the greatest, grandest, most wonderful, loving person in the world because this is what you are going to be giving to your children— to all those you meet.

—LEO BUSCAGLIA

bethedifference

Bringing out your own unique
brand of creativity into your life
and the world can be the most
significant thing you'll ever do.

—LORNA CATFORD, PH.D.

We grow up thinking that the
best answer is in someone else's
brain. Much of our education is an
elaborate game of "guess what's
in the teacher's head?" What the
world really needs to know right
now is what kind of dreams and
ideas are in your head.

—DAN ZADRA

bethedifference

Each of us has a spark of life
inside us, and our highest
endeavor ought to be to set off
that spark in one another.
—KENNY AUSUBEL

Never turn your back on
your own ideas. Make yourself
this one little promise: the next
time you catch yourself saying,
"Hey, that gives me an idea,"
follow through on that idea
to its logical conclusion.
—DAN ZADRA

bethedifference

A gentle reminder to stand up—
and speak up—for your ideals.
Silence is an opinion.

—GIL ATKINSON

I knew someone had to take
the first step and I made up
my mind not to move.

—ROSA PARKS, ON HER DECISION TO SIT IN
THE WHITE'S ONLY SECTION OF THE BUS

Nothing is more beautiful or powerful
than an individual acting out of his
conscience, thus helping to bring
the collective conscience to life.

—NORMAN COUSINS

bethedifference

One person *can* make a difference,
and every person must try.
—JOHN F. KENNEDY

What you will do matters.
All you need is to do it.
—JUDY GRAHN

Each time you
stand up for an ideal,
you send forth a
tiny ripple of hope.
—ROBERT KENNEDY

bethedifference

I believe that one of the most important things to learn in life is that you can make a difference in your community no matter who you are or where you live.

—ROSALYNN CARTER

I have never been especially impressed by the heroics of people convinced that they are about to change the world. I am more awed by those who struggle to make one small difference after another.

—ELLEN GOODMAN

bethedifference

In a nation of millions, and a world of billions, the individual is still the first and basic agent of change.
—LYNDON B. JOHNSON

Few will have the greatness to bend history itself; but each of us can work to change a small portion of events, and in the total of all those acts will be written the history of this generation.
—ROBERT KENNEDY

bethedifference

BELIEVE

*With every rising
of the sun,
think of your life
as just begun.*
—*Unknown*

In the time of your life, live!
—WILLIAM SAROYAN

**One of the illusions is
that the present hour is not
the critical, decisive hour.
Write it on your heart that every
day is the best day of the year.**
—RALPH WALDO EMERSON

**Every moment of your life, including
this one, is a fresh start.**
—B.J. MARSHALL

bethedifference

The tragedy of life is not
that it ends so soon, but that
we wait so long to begin it.

—W.M. LEWIS

Today is your day and mine,
the only day we have, the day
in which we play our part.
What our part may signify in
the great whole, we may not
understand, but we are here
to play it, and now is our time.

—DAVID STARR JORDAN

bethedifference

One day with life and
heart is more than enough
time to find a world.
—JAMES RUSSELL LOWELL

Each dawn holds a new hope
for a new plan, making the start of
each day the start of a new life.
—GINA BLAIR

Always new. Always exciting.
Always full of promise.
The mornings of our lives,
each a personal daily miracle!
—GLORIA GAITHER

bethedifference

Go to the window and
look at the stars.
—GIRAUT DE BORNEIL

Begin doing what you want to do
now. We have only this moment,
sparkling like a star in our hand—
and melting like a snowflake.
—MARIE BEYON RAY

71

Normal day, let me hold you while
I may, for it will not always be so.
One day I shall want more than
all the world your return.
—MARY JEAN IRION

bethedifference

How we spend
our days is, of course,
how we spend our lives.
—ANNIE DILLARD

There's so much speculating
going on that a lot of us never get
around to living. Life is always
walking up to us and saying,
"Come on in, the living's fine,"
and what do we do? Back off
and take its picture.
—RUSSELL BAKER

bethedifference

**Dost thou love life?
Then do not squander time, for
that is the stuff life is made of.**
—BEN FRANKLIN

**Choose life! Only that and
always at whatever risk. To let
life leak out, to let it wear away
by the mere passage of time, to
withhold giving it and spending
it is to choose nothing.**
—SISTER HELEN KELLY

bethedifference

**Think big thoughts
but relish small pleasures.**
—H. JACKSON BROWN, JR.

**Most of us miss out on life's big
prizes, no Pulitzer, Nobel, Oscar
or Emmy. But we're all eligible for
life's small pleasures. A pat on the
back, a kiss behind the ear, a four-
pound bass. A full moon, an empty
parking place, a crackling fire.
A great meal, a glorious sunset.
Enjoy life's tiny delights.
There are plenty for all of us.**
—UNITED TECHNOLOGIES, "GRAY MATTER"

bethedifference

In life, there are no ordinary moments. Most of us never really recognize the most significant moments of our lives when they're happening.

—KATHLEEN MAGEE

Appreciation of life itself, becoming suddenly aware of the miracle of being alive, on this planet, can turn what we call ordinary life into a miracle.

—DAN WAKEFIELD

bethedifference

Sit loosely in the saddle of life.
—ROBERT LOUIS STEVENSON

**Let there be more joy
and laughter in your living.**
—EILEEN CADDY

**If you woke up this morning,
it's time to celebrate!**
—JOE TAKASH

bethedifference

Happiness comes of the
capacity to feel deeply, to
enjoy simply, to think freely,
to risk life, to be needed.
—STORM JAMESON

Worry is a misuse of
your imagination. Live as
many moments as possible
in the quiet, joyous
expectation of good.
—DAN ZADRA

bethedifference

That it will never come again
is what makes life so sweet.
—EMILY DICKINSON

You only live once, but if you
work it right, once is enough.
—JOE E. LEWIS

Special times and special places.
The moments pass so quickly,
but the memories last forever.
—"REMINISCENCES"

bethedifference

Treasure this day,
and treasure yourself.
Truly, neither will ever
happen again.
—RAY BRADBURY

Enjoy yourself. These are
"the good old days" you're
going to miss years ahead.
We can never go back again,
that much is certain.
—B.J. MARSHALL

bethedifference

BELIEVE WH

Do just once what others say you can't do, and you will never pay attention to their limitations again.
—James R. Cook

ENOTHERS
MIGHTNOT

Who are "they" that hold
so much power over our lives?
—ORVILLE THOMPSON

There will be those who will tell you,
you can't make it because of where
you live, because of how you look,
because of the way you talk. We all
have heard that—I almost listened.
—L. DOUGLAS WILDER

To go against the dominant
thinking of your friends, of most
of the people you see every day,
is perhaps the most difficult act
of heroism you can have.
—THEODORE WHITE

bethedifference

Follow your heart even
when others scoff. Don't be
beaten down by naysayers.

—HOWARD SCHULTZ

No one should negotiate
their dreams. Dreams must
be free to flee and fly high.
You should never agree to
surrender your aspirations.

—REV. JESSE JACKSON

There is only one you.
God wanted you to be you.
Don't you dare change just
because you're out-numbered.

—CHARLES SWINDOLL

bethedifference

**Normal is not something
to aspire to, it's something
to get away from.**
—JODIE FOSTER

**Imagination continually
frustrates tradition.
That's its job.**
—JOHN PFEIFFER

**There is nothing more
genuine than breaking away
from the chorus to learn the
sound of your own voice.**
—PO BRANSON

bethedifference

As long as I have to die
my own death, I have decided
to live my own life and not
let others live it for me.
—HANOCH McCARTY

If you're not marching to your own
tune, you're going to be marching to
someone else's. You have to set your
own priorities, or someone will be
happy to set them for you.
—ELIZABETH DOLE

Don't care what others think
of what you do. Care very much
about what you think you do.
—ST. FRANCIS DE SALES

bethedifference

Risk! Risk anything!
Care no more for the opinions
of others, for those voices.
Do the hardest thing on earth
for you. Act for yourself.
—KATHERINE MANSFIELD

At birth, each of us gets a note
slipped under our pillow: "Well, child,
have you the courage—the courage
to be human? Will the ten thousand
things of the world wear you out,
blind you, or break your heart?"
So the test begins; and it is
never complete.
—ERIC MAISEL

bethedifference

Most of the things worth doing
in the world have been declared
impossible before they were done.
—LOUIS D. BRANDEIS

Imagination allows us to
escape the predictable.
It enables us to reply to the
common wisdom that we cannot
soar by saying, "Just watch!"
—BILL BRADLEY

The door that nobody else will
go in at, seems always to swing
open widely for me.
—CLARA BARTON

bethedifference

"Quit now, you'll never make it."
If you disregard this advice,
you'll be halfway there.
—DAVID ZUCKER

Try very hard not to lose
your dream or your ideal.
It is not easy to find it once
you have lost it—the pressure
of life is too strong by then.
—FRANK LLOYD WRIGHT

bethedifference

**Dreams don't die
until we let them.**
—JAMES OJALA

**Obstacles don't make people stop—
people stop themselves.**
—CAROL QUINN

**There exists only one person
who has the power to cast
the deciding vote that will
kill your dream...you!**
—DR. ROBERT SCHULLER

bethedifference

Live your life as an exclamation rather than an explanation.
—UNKNOWN

Changing one small thing for the better is worth more than proving a thousand people wrong.
—ANTHONY PIVEC

When you really get down to it, all that really matters is the work. The work will outlive us and our critics.
—DON HENLEY

bethe**difference**

I can honestly say that I was
never affected by the question
of the success of an undertaking.
If I felt it was the right thing to do,
I was for it regardless of
the possible outcome.

—GOLDA MEIR

We were not created to be eaten
by anxiety, but to walk erect, free,
unafraid in a world where there is
work to do, truth to seek,
love to give and win.

—JOSEPH FORD NEWTON

be the difference

BELIEVETHE
ATTHEENDO

RE'S LIGHT
F THE TUNNEL

*Always know in your heart
that you are far bigger than
anything that can happen
to you.*
—Dan Zadra

There will come a time when
you believe everything is finished.
That will be the beginning.

—LOUIS L'AMOUR

Things don't go from here to
there without passing through
some middle territory.

—RHONDA ABRAMS

There were many ways of breaking
a heart. Stories were full of hearts
broken by love, but what really broke
a heart was taking away its dream—
whatever that dream might be.

—PEARL S. BUCK

bethedifference

It may be that when we no longer
know what to do, we have come
to our real work, and that when we
no longer know which way to go,
we have come to our real journey.
—WENDELL BERRY

When you come to the edge of all
the light you have, and must take a
step into the darkness of the unknown,
believe that one of two things will
happen. Either there will be
something solid for you to stand on—
or you will be taught how to fly.
—PATRICK OVERTON

bethedifference

We define ourselves by the
best that is in us, not the
worst that has been done to us.
—EDWARD LEWIS

I want to know if you can live
with failure, yours and mine,
and still stand on the edge of
the lake and shout to the silver
of the full moon, "Yes!" It doesn't
interest me where or what or with
whom you have studied. I want to
know what sustains you from the
inside when all else falls away.
—ORIAH MOUNTAIN DREAMER

bethedifference

**Don't let the odds
scare you from even trying.**
—HOWARD SCHULTZ

**Unless you walk out into the
unknown, the odds of making
a profound difference in your
life are pretty low.**
—TOM PETERS

**We cannot tell what may happen
to us in the strange medley of life.
But we can decide what happens
in us, how we take it, what we do
with it—and that is what really
counts in the end.**
—JOSEPH FORT NEWTON

bethedifference

**Failure is simply
part of the equation.**
—GEORGETTE MOSBACHER

**Your first big trouble can be
a bonanza if you live through it.
Get through the first trouble
and you'll probably make
it through the next one.**
—RUTH GORDON

**Have faith. Breakdowns
can create breakthroughs.
Things fall apart, so that
things can fall together.**
—DAN ZADRA

bethedifference

Difficulties make you a jewel.
—JAPANESE PROVERB

Hardship often prepares an ordinary person for an extraordinary destiny.
—C.S. LEWIS

Things don't go wrong and break your heart so you can become bitter and give up. They happen to break you down and build you up so you can be all that you were intended to be.
—CHARLES "TREMENDOUS" JONES

bethedifference

Everyday courage has few witnesses. But yours is no less noble because no drum beats before you, and no crowds shout your name.
—ROBERT LOUIS STEVENSON

It gets dark sometimes, but the morning comes. Don't you surrender. Keep hope alive!
—REV. JESSE JACKSON

bethedifference

Doubt is like walking through a
railroad tunnel without a flashlight.
You know daylight is ahead, but
you're tempted to go back through
the darkness to where you began.

—PETER REESE

Hope begins in the dark,
the stubborn hope that if you
just show up and try to do the
right thing, the dawn will come.
You wait and watch and work;
you don't give up.

—ANNE LAMOTT

bethedifference

A great secret of success is
to go through life as someone
who never gets used up.
—ALBERT SCHWEITZER

Here's to the pilot that
weathered the storm.
—GEORGE CANNING

Nobody is stronger than someone
who came back. There is nothing
you can do to such a person
because whatever you could do
is less than what has already
been done to him.
—ELIE WIESEL

bethedifference

Success and failure are
both greatly overrated, but
failure gives you a whole
lot more to talk about.

—HILDEGARD KNEF

One day, in retrospect,
the years of struggle will strike
you as the most beautiful.

—SIGMUND FREUD

Today's trying times in
about twenty years will have
become "the good old days."

—BERNARD MELTZER

bethedifference

BELIEVETHAT
THATLIGHTFOR

I could tell where the lamplighter was by the trail he left behind him.
—Harry Lauder

YOUMAYBE
SOMEONEELSE

We're all here for a reason.
I believe a bit of the reason is
to throw little torches out to
lead people through the dark.

—WHOOPI GOLDBERG

Sometimes our light goes out
but is blown into flame by another
human being. Each of us owes
deepest thanks to those who
have rekindled this light.

—ALBERT SCHWEITZER

bethedifference

To the world you may be just one person, but to one person you may be the world. Make yourself a blessing to someone.

—JOSEPHINE BILLINGS

Too often we underestimate the power of a touch, a smile, a kind word, a listening ear, an honest accomplishment, or the smallest act of caring, all of which have the potential to turn a life around.

—LEO BUSCAGLIA

bethedifference

Each of us has a choice
about how to love the world
in our unique way.
—BERNIE SIEGEL, M.D.

We can all be angels to one another.
We can choose to obey the
still small stirring within,
the little whisper that says,
"Go. Ask. Reach out."
—JOAN WESTER ANDERSON

bethedifference

When you reach out,
the chances are pretty good
that someone will reach back.
—CHERYL RICHARDSON

Just concentrate on helping one
person, giving hope to one person,
and that person in turn may give
hope to somebody else and it
will spread out.
—AARON ABRAHAMSEN

bethedifference

**If you have knowledge,
let others light their candles at it.**
—MARGARET FULLER

**Sometimes the biggest difference
we can make is passing our
wisdom on to someone who will
make a bigger difference.**
—LINDA GRAY

**If you're too busy to
help those around you succeed,
you're too busy.**
—BOB MOAWAD

bethedifference

Friends feed each other's spirits
and dreams and hopes; they feed
each other with the things a
soul needs to live.

—GLEN HARRINGTON-HALL

A friend is someone who knows
the song in your heart, and can
sing it back to you when you have
forgotten the words.

—UNKNOWN

bethedifference

She stood on tip-toe,
atop the tallest mountain,
gathering stars from the
darkening sky because she
knew someone, somewhere
was searching for a source
to light their way.

—LAUREN BOND

Everyone stands alone
at the heart of the world
pierced by a ray of sunlight,
and suddenly it is evening.

—SALVATORE QUASIMODO

bethedifference

All we can ask in our lives is that perhaps we can make a little difference in someone else's.

—LILLIAN DAVIS

If someone can stand on my shoulders and take their dream to a higher level, maybe that's success, too.

—STEVE POTTER

When something comes to life in others because of you, then you have made an approach to immortality.

—NORMAN COUSINS

bethedifference

As we grow older, we discover
that we have two hands:
One for helping ourselves,
the second for helping others.

—UNKNOWN

In the end, I think my greatest
concerns will be, how much love did
I have in my life? How did I share
my love? Who loved me? Whom did I
treasure? Whose lives did I impact?
Did my life make a difference
to someone else?

—RICHARD CARLSON, PH.D.

bethedifference

Someone's sitting in the shade
today because someone planted
a tree a long time ago.
—WARREN BUFFETT

My life now, every minute
of it has the positive meaning
of goodness which I have
the power to put into it.
—KONSTANTINE LEVIN IN "ANNA KARENINA"

Do what you can to show you care
about other people, and you will
make our world a better place.
—ROSALYNN CARTER

bethedifference

BELIEVET
BESTIS

*Come my friends,
'tis not too late
to seek a newer world.*
—*Alfred, Lord Tennyson*

Nobody gets to live life backwards. Look ahead, because that's where your future lies.

—ANN LANDERS

The world ages us too fast. We grow up too quickly, we stop dreaming too early, and we develop the ability to worry at far too young an age.

—DOUG WECKER

bethedifference

**Your imagination is your preview
of life's coming attractions.**
—ALBERT EINSTEIN

**I feel again a spark
of that ancient flame.**
—VIRGIL

**Remember when
you were at your best?
Now be there again!**
—UNKNOWN

bethedifference

Believe in the magic of
tomorrow and your spirits
will be lifted on wings of hope.
—KOBI YAMADA

Each destination you reach
only opens out into wider horizons,
new and undiscovered countries
for you to explore.
—BARBARA SHER WITH ANNIE GOTTLIEB

bethedifference

If you do not think about
the future, you cannot have one.
—JOHN GALSWORTHY

Make your plans as fantastic as
you like, because 25 years from now,
they will seem mediocre. Make your
plans 10 times as great as you first
planned, and 25 years from now you
will wonder why you did not make
them 50 times as great.
—HENRY CURTIS

bethedifference

The reality is that
changes are coming.
They must come. You must
share in bringing them.

—JOHN HERSEY

We are haunted by an
ideal life, and it is because we
have within us the beginning
and the possibility of it.

—PHILLIPS BROOKS

I have seen the future
and it works. Not just for you
and me, but for all of us.

—LINCOLN STEFFENS

bethedifference

We are very near to greatness:
one step and we are safe;
can we not take the leap?
—RALPH WALDO EMERSON

May God bless you with anger
at injustice, so that you will work
for justice, equality and peace.
And may God bless you with the
foolishness to think that you can
make a difference in the world,
so that you will do the things which
others tell you cannot be done.
—UNKNOWN

bethedifference

It is never too late to be
what you might have been.
—GEORGE ELIOT

The old woman I shall
become will be quite different
from the woman I am now.
Another I is beginning.
—GEORGE SAND

The only real aging process
is the erosion of our ideals.
—ALBERT SCHWEITZER

bethedifference

Lord, grant that I may
always desire more than
I can accomplish.
—MICHELANGELO

Can anything be sadder
than work left unfinished?
Yes, work never begun.
—CHRISTINA ROSSETTI

Whatever we have done
with our lives makes us
what we are when we die.
And everything, absolutely
everything counts.
—SOGYAL RINPOCHE

bethedifference

The future belongs to those who believe in the beauty of their dreams. In the long run, we really do shape our own lives; and then together we shape the world around us. The process never ends until we die, and the choices we make are ultimately our responsibility.

—ELEANOR ROOSEVELT

bethedifference

I wish you sunshine on your path
and storms to season your journey.
I wish you peace in the world in which
you live and in the smallest corner of
the heart where truth is kept. More
I cannot wish you, except perhaps
love, to make all the rest worthwhile.
—ROBERT A. WARD

bethedifference

Other "Gift of Inspiration" books available:

Be Happy
Remember to live,
love, laugh and learn

Because of You
Celebrating the
Difference You Make

Brilliance
Uncommon voices from
uncommon women

**Commitment to
Excellence**
Celebrating the Very Best

Diversity
Celebrating the Differences

Everyone Leads
It takes each of us to make
a difference for all of us

Expect Success
Our Commitment
to Our Customer

Forever Remembered
A Gift for the Grieving
Heart

I Believe in You
To your heart, your
dream, and the
difference you make

Little Miracles
Cherished messages
of hope, joy, love,
kindness and courage

Never Quit
Inspiring Insights on
Courage & Commitment

Reach for the Stars
Give up the good
to go for the great

Team Works
Working Together Works

Thank You
In appreciation of you,
and all that you do

To Your Success
Thoughts to Give
Wings to Your Work
and Your Dreams

Together We Can
Celebrating the power
of a team and a dream

We the People
Celebrating the
American Spirit

Welcome Home
Celebrating the
Best Place on Earth

Whatever It Takes
A Journey into the Heart
of Human Achievement

What's Next
Creating the Future Now

You've Got a Friend
Thoughts to Celebrate
the Joy of Friendship